WHAT DOES THE *BIBLE SAY* ABOUT THE FUTURE?

WHAT DOES THE *BIBLE SAY* ABOUT THE FUTURE?

30 Questions on Bible Prophecy, Israel, and the End Times

CHARLES H. DYER

MOODY PUBLISHERS
CHICAGO

Unless otherwise indicated, all Scripture quotations are taken from the (NASB®) New American Standard Bible®, Copyright © 1960, 1971, 1977, 1995, 2020 by The Lockman Foundation. Used by permission. All rights reserved. www.lockman.org

Edited by Elizabeth Cody Newenhuyse
Interior design: Ragont Design
Cover design: Studio Gearbox
Cover image of Jerusalem copyright © 2020 by Kanuman / Shutterstock (404274919). All rights reserved.

Library of Congress Cataloging-in-Publication Data

Names: Dyer, Charles H., 1952- author.
Title: What does the Bible say about the future? : 30 questions on Bible
  prophecy, Israel, and the end times / Dr. Charles H. Dyer.
Description: Chicago : Moody Publishers, [2021] | Includes bibliographical
  references. | Summary: "Don't get caught up in internet speculations and
  doomsday prognostications about the end times. The real place to find
  out about the future is the Word of God. Radio host and prophecy expert
  Dr. Charlie Dyer offers you an insightful look at the end times that's
  grounded in Scripture"-- Provided by publisher.
Identifiers: LCCN 2021043394 (print) | LCCN 2021043395 (ebook) | ISBN
  9780802424471 | ISBN 9780802476982 (ebook)
Subjects: LCSH: Bible--Prophecies--Miscellanea. |
  Bible--Prophecies--Israel--Miscellanea. | Bible--Prophecies--End of the
  world--Miscellanea. | BISAC: RELIGION / Biblical Studies / Prophecy |
  RELIGION / Christian Living / Spiritual Growth
Classification: LCC BS647.3 .D95 2021 (print) | LCC BS647.3 (ebook) | DDC
  220.1/5--dc23
LC record available at https://lccn.loc.gov/2021043394
LC ebook record available at https://lccn.loc.gov/2021043395

Originally delivered by fleets of horse-drawn wagons, the affordable paperbacks from D. L. Moody's publishing house resourced the church and served everyday people. Now after 125 years of publishing and ministry, Moody Publishers' mission remains the same—even if our delivery systems have changed a bit. For more information on other books (and resources) created from a biblical perspective, go to www.moodypublishers.com or write to:

Moody Publishers
820 N. LaSalle Boulevard
Chicago, IL 60610

1 3 5 7 9 10 8 6 4 2

Printed in the United States of America

This book is dedicated to the pastors and staff of Grace Bible Church in Sun City, Arizona. I thank God for the privilege I had of serving our Lord together with you. You occupy a special place in my heart!

"I thank my God in all my remembrance of you."
Philippians 1:3

Contents

Introduction

Political instability. Civil unrest. Financial uncertainty. Erosion of religious liberty. Turmoil in the Middle East. Is it any surprise that some are speculating whether this might be the beginning of the end—that time of worldwide catastrophe predicted in the book of Revelation?

People's responses to all these events have ranged from paralyzing fear to uncontrollable panic to rising indignation and anger. Over the past few years we've received hundreds of questions on *The Land and the Book* radio program asking my opinion on current events. At their most basic level, the questions asked come down to these: How do current events relate to Bible prophecy? Are there signs indicating we are now living in the last days? What does the Bible really say about the future?

Having spent the past decade answering questions sent to *The Land and the Book* radio program, I sense a growing feeling of insecurity about the future on the part of listeners. The purpose of this book is to take you into *the Book* to see what God has really said about future events. Ultimately, I want you to breathe a sigh of relief—and replace fear with faith—as you come to understand how God is still controlling and shaping events in the world today to prepare for the return of His Son.

Follow along as we explore thirty crucial questions about Bible prophecy and its relationship to current events.

1

Are we in the end times/last days?

The answer depends in part on what we mean when we use those terms! If we're referring to the final period of world-wide turmoil just before Jesus returns to earth—the period of time described in Revelation 6–19—then the answer is no. We are not yet in *those* end times.

But in a broader sense the "last days" can refer to the entire period between Christ's first coming and His promised return. In Hebrews 1:2 the writer says the "last days" began at the first coming of Jesus. "[God] in these last days has spoken to us in His Son." But in John 6:40 and 11:24 we're told the resurrection of believing Jews will take place "on the last day," pointing to the time of Jesus' return. Since humanity is still between these two mileposts of history, the period in which we live can be called the last days.

In 1 Timothy 4:1 the apostle Paul warned Timothy about the "later times" when people will "fall away from the faith, paying attention to deceitful spirits and teachings of demons." Then in verse 7 Paul told Timothy to "stay away from" these false teachings, suggesting the "later times" were present since these false teachers were already here. But later, in 2 Timothy 3, Paul pictured a time that would become even more troubling as these last days progress. "But realize this, that in the last days difficult times will come" (v. 1). Paul then lists nineteen specific traits that will characterize humanity as the last days move toward their appointed end.

Peter added one final characteristic of the last days in 2 Peter 3:3–4. He said they will be characterized by the rise of scoffers and mockers who will deny the reality of Jesus' soon return. "Know this first of all, that in the last days mockers will come with their mocking, following after their own lusts, and saying, 'Where is the promise of His coming?'"

The increasing godlessness, pride, brutality, and scoffing pictured by both Paul and Peter suggest the climax of the last days will be a time when much of humanity will shake its fist in the face of God in active rebellion. Based on the description given by Paul and Peter, we could very well be nearing the end of the last days.

The "end times" refers to the specific events associated with the end of the age and the return of Jesus to earth. As the disciples asked on the Mount of Olives, "What will be the sign of Your coming, and of the end of the age?" (Matt. 24:3). We are living in the "last days," but the events associated with the "end times" leading up to Jesus' return have not yet begun. And yet, the curtain on the final act of God's drama could rise at any time!

2

Is Bible prophecy being fulfilled today?

O ver fifty years ago Gordon Jensen wrote "Redemption Draweth Nigh," a song that focused on the second coming of Jesus and that suggested signs pointing to His soon return were "everywhere." But are there signs and prophecies currently being fulfilled that focus directly on the soon return of Jesus?

Some point to the rebirth of Israel as a nation in 1948 as a fulfillment of Ezekiel's prophecy of a valley of dead bones returning to life. "Behold, I am going to open your graves and cause you to come up out of your graves, My people; and I will bring you into the land of Israel" (Ezek. 37:12). Others see prophecy being fulfilled in modern Israel's transformation of the land. "The wilderness and the desert will rejoice, and the desert will shout for joy and blossom; like the crocus it will blossom profusely" (Isa. 35:1–2). But are these actual fulfillments of Bible prophecy?

The problem is that many people understand the fulfillment of prophecy in much the same way they understand romantic love. They claim to "know it when they see it," but they can't provide a clear explanation of what "it" actually is. A prophecy has only one meaning, though it can have multiple applications. The best way to determine if a prophecy has been fulfilled is first to understand what the original prophecy actually predicted. Only then can we look to see if current events match that prediction.

The rebirth of Israel as a nation in 1948 doesn't actually fulfill Ezekiel's prophecy. Ezekiel's vision described both a physical restoration (bones coming back together) and a spiritual rebirth (causing God's breath to enter the still-dead bodies) of the nation. But when God interpreted the vision, He said the spiritual rebirth would occur at the same time as the physical restoration. "I will put My Spirit within you and you will come to life, and I will place you on your own land" (Ezek. 37:14). The spiritual restoration of Israel hasn't yet happened, so the prophecy hasn't yet been fulfilled.

While we're not yet seeing the fulfillment of these prophecies, we could very well be seeing God setting the stage for His end-time program. The distinction is subtle, but important. The final act in God's prophetic drama hasn't yet begun. The curtain remains down. But from our seats we hear the sound of props being moved into place and the muffled coughs of actors preparing to play their designated roles. This suggests the curtain could soon rise as the drama begins to unfold.

Guard against finding the fulfillment of Bible prophecy in every current event.

But remember, the actual fulfillment of end-time events hasn't yet begun.

The nation of Israel is back in the land because the final act in God's prophetic drama revolves around them. The land itself has experienced a renewal, but they have yet to see "the glory of the LORD, the majesty of our God" (Isa. 35:2), which is also part of Isaiah's prediction.

Guard against finding the fulfillment of Bible prophecy in every current event. Those who have done so in the past have found themselves looking foolish when the "fulfillments" evaporated. During World War II some were convinced Hitler was the prophesied Antichrist, Mussolini was the false prophet, and Japan fulfilled the prediction regarding the kings from the east.

Be cautious about claiming Bible prophecies are being fulfilled today. The prophecy will only be "fulfilled" when all the details of the prophecy come to pass.

Are natural disasters,
like earthquakes and plagues,
a fulfillment of Bible prophecy?

The Old Testament word for plague (*nega'*) originally referred to the physical blow a ruler would deliver as punishment. Most of the time in the Old Testament it was used to refer to God sending a physical judgment or disease. The plagues God sent against Egypt included physical sufferings, like boils or the death of the firstborn son; but most were external judgments like frogs, lice, locusts, hail, or intense darkness. In Ezekiel 5:12 and 6:12 the prophet connected the word "plague" with physical disease that would kill those inside Jerusalem. "A third of you will die by plague or perish by famine among you, a third will fall by the sword around you, and a third I will scatter to every wind, and I will unsheathe a sword behind them" (Ezek. 5:12).

The English word "plague" comes from the Greek word *plēgē*, which describes a plague, blow, or wound. In the book of Revelation the plagues associated with the seven trumpets and seven bowls include earthquakes and other physical destruction on parts of the earth, demonic attacks, physical diseases, and intense heat and darkness (Rev. 9; 16).

God did send both earthquakes and physical disease as judgment for sin, though these weren't the only kinds of plagues He used to punish individuals. This leads to an important question. How do we know if an earthquake or plague is actually intended as a divine judgment to fulfill Bible prophecy? Job experienced loss of property and intense physical illness. His three friends were convinced Job was experiencing all this distress as judgment from the hand of God, but the reader is taken behind the scenes in chapters 1–2 to discover this was not the case. The friends were wrong!

In the absence of a direct, divine prediction, anyone assuming a specific disaster was sent as divine judgment is actually presuming on God.

Apart from God raising up a prophet to announce it in advance, we have no way of knowing if such a natural disaster was sent from God as judgment. Amos was sent to announce God's judgment "two years before the earthquake" (Amos 1:1). But in the absence of a direct, divine prediction, anyone assuming a specific disaster was sent as divine judgment is actually presuming on God, just as Job's friends had done. Jesus used the illustration of a catastrophic tower collapse that killed eighteen people in Jerusalem to make a similar point in His day. "Or do you think that those eighteen on whom the tower in Siloam fell and killed them were worse offenders than all the other people who live in Jerusalem? No, I tell you" (Luke 13:4–5).

In theory someone could come forward claiming to be a prophet of God and announce that a coming natural disaster is God's divine judgment. But that individual had better be sure he or she is indeed a true prophet being sent by God, because God set a very high standard for those claiming to speak in His name. "When the prophet speaks in the name of the LORD, and the thing does not happen or come true, that is the thing which the LORD has not spoken. The prophet has spoken it presumptuously" (Deut. 18:22). And two verses earlier God explained what was to be done to someone speaking "presumptuously" in His name. "But the prophet who speaks a word presumptuously in My name, a word which I have not commanded him to speak . . . shall die" (Deut. 18:20).

Does the temple need to be rebuilt before the end times can begin? If so, what will happen to the Dome of the Rock?

The Bible says a rebuilt temple in Jerusalem will play a role in end-time events. Daniel 9:24–27 describes a final seven-year period just prior to the Messiah coming to set up His kingdom. In the middle of this seven-year period Daniel is told of a coming "prince" who will "put a stop to sacrifice and grain offering." In their place "on the wing of abominations will come the one who makes desolate" (v. 27). For this to happen, the sacrificial system must be in operation. In Matthew 24:15–16 Jesus refers back to Daniel's prophecy. "Therefore when you see the ABOMINATION OF DESOLATION which was spoken of through Daniel the prophet, standing in the holy place—let the reader understand—then those who are in Judea must flee to the mountains." Jesus makes it clear that the abomination will be set up in the "holy place," which refers to the temple.

In 2 Thessalonians 2:3–4 Paul explains the activity of the future Antichrist. "No one is to deceive you in any way! For it will not come unless the apostasy comes first, and the man of lawlessness is revealed, the son of destruction, who opposes and exalts himself above every so-called god or object of worship, so that he takes his seat in the temple of God, displaying himself as being God." The Antichrist will go to "the temple of God" to proclaim himself as God. For that to happen, a temple must be built.

The final passage that points to a future temple is Revelation 11:1–2. "Then there was given to me a measuring rod like a staff; and someone said, 'Get up and measure the temple of God and the altar, and those who worship in it. Leave out the courtyard which is outside the temple and do not measure it, because it has been given to the nations; and they will trample the holy city for forty-two months.'" John wrote the book of Revelation around AD 95, twenty-five years after the destruction of the temple in Jerusalem. He is told to measure a future temple that will exist in Jerusalem for at least a three-and-a-half-year period.

A temple must be present during the tribulation period, but it doesn't need to exist prior to the start of that period. These passages simply require the temple to be in existence by the middle of that final seven-year period. Interestingly, construction on the second temple began on September 21, 520 BC (Hag. 1:14–15) and was completed on March 12, 516 BC (Ezra 6:15)—a construction period lasting almost exactly three-and-a-half years. If the second temple could be built in that length of time, so can a future temple!

Where will this temple be built? The basic answer is that it will be built where the orthodox Jews believe the last temple stood. Archaeologically that's almost certainly where the Dome of the Rock now stands. However, there are those who believe the temple actually stood just to the north of the Dome of the Rock and who have drawn up plans showing that the temple and inner court could be rebuilt without disturbing the Dome of the Rock or the Al-Aqsa Mosque.[1] Could this be what God meant when He told John, "Leave out the courtyard which is outside the temple and do not measure it, because it has been given to the nations" (Rev. 11:2)?

We don't yet know how the Jewish people will be able to build their temple. But thankfully, God does!

Do the ark of the covenant and the red heifer need to be found before the end times can begin?

Both of these are connected to the rebuilding of the temple, but the short answer is that neither is required before the end times can begin. Different people have suggested the ark of the covenant is currently hidden in Ethiopia, or the Judean Wilderness, or somewhere in Jordan, or underneath the Temple Mount. (And, of course, Hollywood has it boxed up in a warehouse in Washington, DC!) But the simple truth is that the ark of the covenant disappeared from history about the time of the Babylonian captivity in 586 BC and will never make another appearance here on earth again.

The last historical reference to the ark of the covenant was a command given by King Josiah in 2 Chronicles 35:3. Apparently the ark was being carried about by the Levites, either to hide it for safekeeping during the reigns of Manasseh and Amon or to somehow put it on display or share it with the nation. But in 622 BC Josiah instituted a series of religious reforms, including a firm command regarding the ark of the covenant. "Put the holy ark in the house which Solomon the son of David king of Israel built; it will not be a burden on your shoulders."

Thirty-six years later the ark vanished from history. While some believe it was somehow spirited away by Jeremiah or others, the reality is far less dramatic. In 592 BC Ezekiel saw a vision of

God's shekinah glory leaving the temple (Ezek. 10:1–22; 11:22–24). From that point on, the ark of the covenant was nothing more than a gold-covered box. And when the Babylonians captured Jerusalem, they likely took it along as booty and eventually melted it down.

Jeremiah predicted that the ark would *not* be part of a future temple. "'And it shall be in those days when you become numerous and are fruitful in the land,' declares the LORD, 'they will no longer say, "The ark of the covenant of the LORD." And it will not come to mind, nor will they remember it, nor miss it, nor will it be made again'" (Jer. 3:16). When Israel came back from captivity, the ark wasn't included with the temple furnishings they brought along with them. And when the second temple was finally built, the ark was not present. As Josephus wrote, "But the inmost part of the temple of all was of twenty cubits. This was also separated from the outer part by a veil. *In this there was nothing at all.*"[2]

The ark of the covenant wasn't needed before the second temple was built, and it won't be needed again for a new temple.

The ashes of a red heifer, however, *are* needed before any temple services can resume! In Numbers 19 God explained the purpose for these ashes. They were "to remove impurity" and to provide "purification from sin" (v. 9). To serve in the temple, a priest needs to be ritually pure, and that can't happen until a red heifer is found and its ashes are prepared.

Technically, the more proper color for this animal might be auburn or brown. Ancient Hebrew didn't have different words to distinguish these shades. They would all be classified as "red." But whatever its exact color, the cow has to be physically perfect. It can't have so much as two hairs of a different color.

Before a new temple can be built, Jewish religious leaders believe they either need to find the jar with the ashes of the last red heifer . . . or prepare ashes from a new red heifer. Different groups have spent years trying to breed a red heifer. There is sufficient time for such a cow to be raised, verified, and sacrificed once the end times begin. So the red heifer doesn't necessarily have to be found before the start of that period.

6

Is Israel still God's chosen nation, or have they been replaced by the church?

Israel is central to God's program for the future and has *not* been replaced by the church. God made a promise to Abraham and his descendants in Genesis 12:3 that is still in effect. "And I will bless those who bless you, and the one who curses you I will curse. And in you all the families of the earth will be blessed."

Replacement theology, the belief that the church has replaced Israel, misses the mark when it comes to what God has promised to the Jewish people. There is only one section in the Bible where the writer specifically addresses the issue of the relationship between the church and Israel—Romans 9–11. Paul does say that during the current age the Jewish people have been broken off from the place of blessing and that the Gentiles have been grafted in (Rom. 11:17). However, Paul also includes two other important truths. First, he makes it clear that the rejection was not *total* because Jewish people (including Paul himself) are still coming to faith (11:1–6). And second, he also makes it clear that the rejection is not *permanent* because a day will come when all Israel will be saved (11:25–26).

Paul connects Israel's full salvation to the return of the Messiah (11:26–28), and

Both Israel and the church are "chosen people" in the sense that God has formed a special relationship with both groups.

he is confident it will take place because, he writes, "the gifts and the calling of God are irrevocable" (11:29). God doesn't renege on His promises . . . either to the Jewish people or to the church. Our hope of heaven is grounded in the promises God has made to us. If God can break His promises to the Jewish people, then what assurance do we have that He will not break the promises He has made to us? That's the point Paul is making, and it's a very strong argument for seeing God's promises to Israel as still applying to the Jewish people.

Both Israel and the church are "chosen people" in the sense that God has formed a special relationship with both groups. The point at which they intersect is at Jesus and His death on the cross. That is the basis for both groups experiencing forgiveness of sin and, ultimately, the complete fulfillment of all God's promised blessings.

We also need to realize that God's selection of the Jewish people was not just to a place of special favor but also to a place of special service. When God called Abraham, He said that all nations would be blessed through him. Rather than dealing directly with all humanity as He had been doing prior to the Tower of Babel, God now chose to mediate His blessing to the world through Abraham and his descendants. God revealed His written Word to them, and God called them to be a light to the nations. It's true that with the responsibility also came God's promised blessing. Paul describes some of those blessings in Romans 9:4–5. But the stress in the Old Testament was on the responsibility God placed on His chosen people.

It might help to think of this in terms of the parallel promises God has made to the church. Some might argue that God's promises to the church smack of favoritism in the sense that He has chosen some for salvation while not choosing others. Just as the church is God's elect and beloved, so God has also made similar promises in regard to the nation of Israel. The best way to end this debate (both for Israel and for the church) is to focus on the words Paul used to end his discussion in Romans 11:33–36. The depth of God's wisdom and knowledge extends far beyond anything we can imagine. We might not understand why He selected the Jewish people, or why He selected us. But we have to trust that He knows best and that what He did was part of His amazing plan for His creation.

What role does Israel play in God's program for the future?

In Daniel 9:24–27 God announced that 490 years (seventy groups of seven years) remained to be fulfilled in the unfolding of God's prophetic program for Israel leading up to the establishment of the kingdom. The goal of this time period is to "finish the wrongdoing, to make an end of sin, to make atonement for guilt, to bring in everlasting righteousness, to seal up vision and prophecy, and to anoint the Most Holy Place" (v. 24). The first 483 years focused on the time period leading up to the coming of the Messiah. The final seven years will complete God's program, resulting in the establishment of the kingdom. But it's crucial to note that Daniel is told the entire 490-year period is for "your people [the Jews] and your holy city [Jerusalem]."

During the final seven-year period, Jerusalem will be the focus of the world, but not in a good sense. The nations of the world will seek to eliminate Israel and overrun Jerusalem:

"Behold, I am going to make Jerusalem a cup that causes staggering to all the peoples around; and when the siege is against Jerusalem, it will also be against Judah. It will come about on that day that I will make Jerusalem a heavy stone for all the peoples; all who lift it will injure themselves severely. And all the nations of the earth will be gathered against it" (Zech. 12:2–3).

God's future for Israel centers on the return of the Messiah and the establishment of His promised Kingdom. This was the universal prediction of virtually all the Old Testament prophets. Here are several examples.

- **Isaiah 9:7**—"There will be no end to the increase of His government or of peace on the throne of David and over his kingdom, to establish it and to uphold it with justice and righteousness from then on and forevermore. The zeal of the LORD of armies will accomplish this."

- **Jeremiah 33:14–15, 25–26**—"'Behold, days are coming,' declares the LORD, 'when I will fulfill the good word which I have spoken concerning the house of Israel and the house of Judah. In those days and at that time I will make a righteous Branch of David sprout; and He shall execute justice and righteousness on the earth.' . . . This is what the LORD says: 'If My covenant for day and night does not continue, and I have not established the fixed patterns of heaven and earth, then I would reject the descendants of Jacob and David My servant, so as not to take from his descendants rulers over the descendants of Abraham, Isaac, and Jacob. But I will restore their fortunes and have mercy on them.'"

- **Ezekiel 37:21–22**—"This is what the Lord GOD says: 'Behold, I am going to take the sons of Israel from among the nations where they have gone, and I will gather them from every side and bring them into their own land; and I will make them one nation in the land, on the mountains of Israel; and one king will be king for all of them; and they will no longer be two nations, and no longer be divided into two kingdoms.'"

- **Daniel 2:44**—"In the days of those kings the God of heaven will set up a kingdom which will never be destroyed, and that kingdom will not be left for another people; it will crush and put an end to all these kingdoms, but it will itself endure forever."

- **Daniel 7:27**—"Then the sovereignty, the dominion, and the greatness of all the kingdoms under the whole heaven will be given to the people of the saints of the Highest One; His kingdom will be an everlasting kingdom, and all the empires will serve and obey Him."
- **Micah 4:8**—"As for you, tower of the flock, hill of the daughter of Zion, to you it will come—yes, the former dominion will come, the kingdom of the daughter of Jerusalem."

If someone accepts these passages at face value, they predict a future earthly kingdom promised by God to Israel. Here are some reasons I believe taking such passages literally—or at face value—is the best approach.

- It offers a consistent approach to interpreting the Bible. The normal, grammatical, literary approach guards against spiritualizing or reading someone's own thoughts into the text. The passage means what it says, not what an individual can somehow spiritualize it to mean.
- A literal reading of the text consistently presents a clear distinction between Israel and the church. As noted earlier, the only section specifically written to explain the relationship between the two is Romans 9–11. And in that section Paul states clearly that there is a future for Israel, which he connects to the return of Christ.
- The prophecies related to the first coming of Christ were all fulfilled literally. That provides a pattern for how we ought to interpret those prophecies related to His second coming.

8

What's the next event on God's prophetic calendar? How can we be so sure?

From New Testament times until now, the next event to be fulfilled on God's prophetic timetable is the return of Jesus for His church. This is the event Paul describes in 1 Thessalonians 4, an event we often call the rapture. Paul announced that the "dead in Christ will rise first. Then we who are alive, who remain, will be caught up together with them in the clouds to meet the Lord in the air" (vv. 16–17). Paul actually expected this to happen in his lifetime, which is why he included himself among those who would be alive when it happened. The event didn't occur in Paul's lifetime, and it hasn't yet taken place. That means it still remains item #1 on God's to-do list for the future. Once God removes the church from the earth, then He will take up His final seven-year prophetic timetable for the nation of Israel.

We can be confident this is the next event because of the distinction the Bible makes between God's program for Israel and His program for the church. In Revelation 1–3 John talks about the church, focusing on Jesus' seven letters to the seven churches. In chapters 4–5 John pictures a great scene around God's throne in heaven. Then beginning in chapter 6, and going through chapter 19, John records the events that lead up to the return of Christ to earth. Once John begins focusing on those future events, the word "church" disappears from the book. Instead John describes

"144,000, sealed from every tribe of the sons of Israel" (7:4–8), two prophets who parallel Moses and Elijah prophesying in Jerusalem (11:3–6), and "a woman clothed with the sun, and the moon under her feet, and on her head a crown of twelve stars" (12:1). The vision comes from Joseph's dream in Genesis 37:9–10, where it pictured Jacob and his sons. In Revelation the vision is describing the nation of Israel being persecuted by Satan.

The key point here is that once John begins describing end-time events leading up to the return of Jesus, the prophetic spotlight shifts from the church to Israel and Jerusalem. Confusing God's programs for the two groups can even cause followers of Jesus to succumb to fear and uncertainty. In 2 Thessalonians the church had received a message, supposedly from Paul, telling them they were already in the day of the Lord. Paul calmed their hearts by first reminding them of the order of future events, which he had taught while with them (2:3–12). He then reminded them that our destiny as believers is to be saved/delivered through the work of the Spirit in our lives, and he encouraged them to remember that teaching and to stand firm (2:13–15).

Evidently people were so certain the end times were upon them that they had stopped working and were just waiting for the end to come.

People often stop at the end of 2 Thessalonians 2, as if the chapter break indicates a change in subject. But pay careful attention to what Paul then says in chapter 3, because it connects with the previous chapter. Evidently people were so certain the end times were upon them that they had stopped working and were just waiting for the end to come. Paul reminds them that when he was in Thessalonica teaching them about the end times he still kept working so as to be a model to them on how they ought to live as they wait for the Lord to come (3:6–9). Paul then gives one very practical piece of advice that he had evidently also shared with them earlier. "If anyone is not willing to work, then he is not to eat, either" (v. 10). Those who were so wrapped up in a frenzy of end-time speculation that it was impacting their normal day-to-day routine were not to be encouraged in such behavior. Like the signs at National Parks warning people not to feed the animals, Paul's practical way of encouraging these believers was to tell everyone else not to feed them so they would go back to living a God-honoring lifestyle!

9

Will people have a second chance to be saved after the rapture?

This question is based on a misunderstanding of events following the rapture. We like to assume that those who have not yet placed their faith in Christ will watch those events unfold and finally say to themselves, "This is what God predicted. It's coming to pass. I'd be foolish now not to trust in Christ, because I know what's going to happen." But in Revelation 9:20 John writes, "The rest of mankind, who were not killed by these plagues, did not repent of the works of their hands." In the end, people have to choose whether or not they believe what God has said, even when the events are clearly taking place. And sadly, many will choose not to believe. This has been true in the past, it's true today, and it will also be true in the future.

In 2 Thessalonians Paul writes that in the coming tribulation period Satan will use "all power and false signs and wonders, and with all the deception of wickedness for those who perish" (2:9–10a). Satan will employ every means possible to trick and deceive those still living on earth into accepting his false narrative. Paul then sadly concludes people will perish "because they did not accept the love of the truth so as to be saved. For this reason God will send upon them a deluding influence so that they will believe what is false" (vv. 10b–11). The sinfulness of the human heart, coupled with Satan's grand deception and God's supernatural hardening, will be enough to effectively blind most to the truth of what has actually happened.

While it appears as if those who have deliberately rejected Christ won't have a second chance to accept Him following the rapture, only God knows the condition of the human heart.

I see at least one historic parallel that might help us understand this reality more clearly. The Bible predicted the exact time of the Messiah's first coming (Dan. 9:24–26). It also announced where He would be born (Mic. 5:2), predicted that He would arrive in Jerusalem riding on a colt (Zech. 9:9), and stated that He would die with the wicked, be buried with the rich, and yet somehow prolong His days (Isa. 53). In fact, there were *scores* of other direct, dramatic prophecies fulfilled at Christ's first coming. But in spite of all these clear prophecies, the religious leaders in that day still chose to disregard them as they condemned Him to death. This is a good example of how prophecy, even when it was clearly known, could still be disregarded. The same thing will be true in the future, especially for those who have knowingly heard and rejected the claims of Christ.

Thankfully, the situation isn't totally hopeless. While it appears that those who have deliberately and knowingly rejected Christ won't have a second chance to accept Him following the rapture, only God knows the condition of the human heart. Someone might appear to have totally rejected the gospel message but not completely closed their heart to God's prompting in their life. Many have heard the gospel message countless times without responding, only to "have the light come on" the next time the gospel is presented. They hadn't so much *rejected* the claims of Jesus as simply been *blind* to the truth of the message. So it's possible that some who have heard the gospel prior to the rapture will hear and respond to the message afterward.

In addition, millions who have never heard the gospel message will have the opportunity to hear and respond during the tribulation period. Revelation 7:9 describes "a great multitude which no one could count, from every nation and all the tribes, peoples, and languages, standing before the throne and before the Lamb." An angel explains to John who they are. "These are the ones who come out of the great tribulation, and they have washed their robes and made them white in the blood of the Lamb" (7:14). Believers from around the world will come to faith. That's the good news. The not-so-good news is that many of them will be martyred during the tribulation period. The price tag for following Jesus during this time will be quite high. Yet, thankfully, many will respond.

10

What are the "signs of the time" mentioned by Jesus in Matthew 24, and are they happening today?

Matthew 24 is a crucial passage for Bible prophecy because it contains Jesus' teaching about the future. The passage begins with the disciples pausing on the Mount of Olives to point out the temple buildings to Jesus. Jesus responded by announcing "not one stone here will be left upon another" (v. 2). This confused the disciples because they thought Jesus had come as Israel's Messiah to defeat Rome and set up the kingdom. They were expecting a Jewish *triumph*, but He announced an impending Jewish *tragedy*.

The disciples then asked Jesus two questions. "Tell us, when will these things happen, and what will be the sign of Your coming, and of the end of the age?" (v. 3). The first question focused on *when* the events would happen, and the second focused on the *sign* that would indicate the time had arrived. Jesus answered the two questions in reverse order. He first described all the signs leading up to the "sign of the Son of Man," which refers to His actual appearance (v. 30). After focusing on the *second* question (relating to the *sign*), Jesus then addressed their *first* question (relating to the issue of *when* He would come). We need to look at His answer in detail.

Jesus began by focusing on signs related to the general characteristics of the age leading up to His return (vv. 4–14). While some believe these signs describe the entire period between His first and second comings, a period of time that long wouldn't be very helpful as a sign. Certainly over the course of hundreds or thousands of years one would expect the arrival of false messiahs, wars, famines, earthquakes, and persecution. Because Jesus said these were "merely the beginning of birth pains" (v. 8), it's possible to see these signs as nothing more than a description of the general trouble and difficulty that would continue throughout the period. Understood that way, they simply become the prophetic "background noise" or static characterizing the entire period.

They were expecting an impending Jewish *triumph*, but He announced an impending Jewish *tragedy*.

However, it's also possible Jesus was referring to specific events in the first half of the final seven-year tribulation period. Rather than simply providing general characteristics of the entire age between the two advents, Jesus would then be describing specific conditions that will characterize the beginning of that coming seven-year period. This seems likely since the signs described by Jesus actually parallel the first five seal judgments in Revelation 6. And if they are parallel, then the signs are *not* being fulfilled today.

MATTHEW 24:4–14	REVELATION 6:1–11
Rise of false messiahs (24:4–5)	Rise of the Antichrist (6:1–2)
Wars and rumors of wars (24:6–7a)	Peace taken from the earth (6:3–4)
Famines and earthquakes (24:7b–8)	Famine (6:5–6)
No parallel	Death of a quarter of the earth's population (6:7–8)
Persecution and martyrdom (24:9–14)	Martyrdom (6:9–11)

Having provided the general conditions His followers could expect during this period, Jesus then gives a very specific sign that will signal the beginning of the time of great persecution. "Therefore when you see the ABOMINATION OF DESOLATION which was spoken of through Daniel the prophet, standing in the holy place—let the reader understand—then those who are in Judea must flee to the mountains. Whoever is on the housetop must not go down to get things out of his house. And whoever is in the field must not turn back to get his cloak. But woe to those women who are pregnant, and to those who are nursing babies in those days! Moreover, pray that when you flee, it will not be in the winter, or on a Sabbath. For then there will be a great tribulation, such as has not occurred since the beginning of the world until now, nor ever will again" (Matt. 24:15–21).

The "ABOMINATION OF DESOLATION" is a reference to Daniel 9:27, which marks the midpoint of the final seven-year period remaining on God's prophetic timeline for Israel. It also signals the start of a three-and-a-half-year period of tremendous persecution. In fact, Jesus said, "If those days had not been cut short, no life would have been saved" (Matt. 24:22). This is a major sign that will require an immediate response on the part of those who witness it. Any delay—even to return home for a coat—could have deadly consequences.

Jesus continues His description of this final period of time by reminding His followers not to believe the many reports of "false christs and false prophets" (v. 24). The age will end with supernatural signs in the heavens. "But immediately after the tribulation of those days THE SUN WILL BE DARKENED, AND THE MOON WILL NOT GIVE ITS LIGHT, AND THE STARS WILL FALL from the sky, and the powers of the heavens will be shaken" (v. 29). And then Jesus presents the final sign that will signal the end of the age. "And then the sign of the Son of Man will appear in the sky, and then all the tribes of the earth will mourn, and they will see the SON OF MAN COMING ON THE CLOUDS OF THE SKY with power and great glory" (v. 30).

In context, the "signs of the times" described by Jesus are the signs that will occur throughout the final seven-year period of time still remaining to fulfill God's prophetic program for Israel. But this shouldn't surprise us. From the call of Moses in the book of Exodus through this final period of time before the arrival of the Messiah, God has used signs as a means of confirming His revelation to the Jewish people (1 Cor. 1:22).

11

How do we know Christians won't go through the tribulation period?

Christians will not go through that seven-year period of time often called the tribulation because according to Daniel 9:24, that period of time is uniquely for "your people [the Jews] and your holy city [Jerusalem]." Now this *doesn't* mean Christians won't experience persecution. Persecution has been the norm for Christians throughout most of the church age. In John 16:33 Jesus warned His disciples, "In the world you have tribulation." Saints in all ages ought to expect opposition to their faith and even persecution.

But the Bible is clear in teaching that Christians won't be part of the final seven-year time of worldwide trouble that immediately precedes Christ's return to earth because the entire prophecy of Daniel 9 was for the Jewish people. That was true of the first 483 years of the prophecy, and it will also be true of the final seven. This is a time when God begins dealing with Israel in a very special and unique way.

In Matthew 24 Jesus mentioned the abomination of desolation spoken of by Daniel the prophet in Daniel 9:27. The passage describes end-time events that climax in His return to earth. After describing the abomination of desolation (v. 15), Jesus says, "Then those who are in *Judea* must flee to the mountains" (v. 16, emphasis added). He also tells the individuals alive at that time to "pray that when you flee, it will not be in the winter, or on a *Sabbath*"

(v. 20, emphasis added). Jesus is connecting this dramatic event with the land of Judea . . . and the Jewish Sabbath.

In 1 Thessalonians 4 Paul describes the rapture of the church. Then in chapter 5 he describes the events of the day of the Lord. But Paul introduces the day of the Lord with the Greek phrase *peri de* ("Now as to . . . "). Paul uses this phrase eight times in his writings—twice in 1 Thessalonians (4:9; 5:1) and six times in 1 Corinthians (7:1, 25; 8:1; 12:1; 16:1, 12). In every instance, he uses it to introduce a new topic. Pay careful attention to Paul's order of topics in 1 Thessalonians. Christ comes to remove His church from the earth (chapter 4). New topic (*peri de*). Here's what will happen in the day of the Lord (chapter 5). The day of the Lord, a time of trouble, follows the rapture of the church.

The book of Revelation also makes a distinction between the church and Israel. In His letter to the faithful church in Philadelphia Jesus promises, "Because you have kept My word of perseverance, I also will keep you from the hour of the testing, that hour which is about to come upon the whole world, to test those who live on the earth" (3:10). The "hour of the testing" relates to the events described in Revelation 6–19, events leading up to the second coming of Christ to earth. Jesus doesn't promise to keep these faithful believers *through* the tribulation or *in* the tribulation. He promises to keep them *from* the very time period when these events will happen.

Jesus' promise in Revelation 3:10 helps us understand the relationship of the church to Israel through the book of Revelation. The word "church" occurs frequently in chapters 1–3, but it then disappears from the chapters that describe the end-time events leading up to Jesus' return (6–19). In place of the church we are told about 144,000 from the twelve tribes of Israel (ch. 7);

two witnesses in Jerusalem (ch. 11); a vision of a woman clothed with the sun, moon, and twelve stars (ch. 12, taken from Joseph's dream in Genesis 37); and a gathering at Megiddo in preparation for the final battle (Rev. 16).

By putting all these pieces together, it seems clear that the rapture occurs when Jesus returns in the air to remove the church from the earth and take it to heaven. That event will be followed by the final seven-year period described in Daniel 9:27, which is when God will fulfill His remaining prophecies related to Israel in preparation for the return of His Son. The church should expect to undergo tribulation here on earth, but the church will not go through the seven-year tribulation period, because it's a time when God will again be dealing in a unique way with the nation of Israel.

12

What is the "time
of Jacob's distress"?

The "time of Jacob's distress" refers to the future tribulation period, especially the second half of that period when Israel will be persecuted by the Antichrist.

The phrase is used by the prophet Jeremiah to describe this period of intense persecution just before Israel's final restoration. "'For behold, days are coming,' declares the LORD, 'when I will restore the fortunes of My people Israel and Judah.' The LORD says, 'I will also bring them back to the land that I gave to their forefathers, and they shall take possession of it. . . . Woe, for that day is great, there is none like it; and it is the time of Jacob's distress, yet he will be saved from it'" (Jer. 30:3, 7). Though the prophet wrote these words before the Babylonian captivity, he was looking beyond Judah's restoration from Babylon to a time when both Israel and Judah will be rescued, restored to the land, and joined to their God in a new covenant relationship.

In chapters 30–33 Jeremiah uses the phrases "days are coming," "that day," "in days to come," "those days," "latter days," or "at that time" twelve times to tie together this time of persecution with the final physical and spiritual restoration of both Israel and Judah (Jer. 30:3, 7, 8, 24; 31:27, 29, 31, 33, 38; 33:14–16). The period of persecution will be followed by the rebuilding of Jerusalem and the inauguration of a new covenant. Though Jeremiah is the only writer to refer to this future period of persecution as the "time of Jacob's distress," other writers do describe the same episode of persecution and trouble that will occur just prior to the return of Jesus and the establishment of God's kingdom.

Daniel wrote about the rise of an end-time king who will "exalt himself and boast against every god and will speak dreadful things against the God of gods" (Dan. 11:36). The prophet then pictured a time of terrible persecution for the Jewish people. "Now at that time Michael, the great prince who stands guard over the sons of your people, will arise. And there will be a time of distress such as never occurred since there was a nation until that time; and at that time your people, everyone who is found written in the book, will be rescued" (Dan. 12:1). Daniel wrote this *after* the people of Judah had begun returning from Babylonian captivity, indicating this time of persecution was still in the future.

Five hundred years after Daniel, Jesus also described this future time of persecution for the Jewish people and said it would be unparalleled in its ferocity. "Therefore when you see the ABOMINATION OF DESOLATION which was spoken of through Daniel the prophet, standing in the holy place—let the reader understand—then those who are in Judea must flee to the mountains. . . . For then there will be a great tribulation, such as has not occurred since the beginning of the world until now, nor ever will again" (Matt. 24:15–16, 21). Jesus associated this future time of trouble with the final three-and-a-half years of Daniel's prophecy in Daniel 9:27. And He indicates this time of "tribulation" will only end when He returns to earth to set up His kingdom.

In the book of Revelation the apostle John also describes this time of future persecution. It will be a time when Satan actively seeks to destroy the Jewish people, pictured as a woman clothed with the sun, the moon under her feet, a crown of twelve stars on her head—a figurative picture of Israel drawn from the dream of young Joseph in Genesis 37:9–10. "Then the woman fled into the wilderness where she had a place prepared by God, so that there she would be nourished for 1,260 days. . . . And when the dragon saw that he was thrown down to the earth, he persecuted the woman who gave birth to the male Child. But the two wings of the great eagle were given to the woman, so that she could fly into the wilderness to her place, where she was nourished for a time, times, and half a time, away from the presence of the serpent" (Rev. 12:6, 13–14).

13

What is the prophecy of Gog and Magog in Ezekiel 38–39? Is it a Russian invasion of Israel?

The battle described in Ezekiel 38–39 occurs at a time when Israel is back in the land, apparently living in peace and safety. From the day Ezekiel penned these words until today, there has never been an attack against Israel by the coalition of nations pictured in this prophecy. Though the names of the nations listed by Ezekiel aren't found on modern maps, they were real countries in Ezekiel's day. The leader is an empire builder named *Gog*. The name harkens back to a ruthless king named Gyges who ruled in what is today western Turkey, less than a century before Ezekiel. Gyges was associated with tyranny and conquest, which is why Ezekiel uses his name to picture this future ruler. It would be similar to someone today describing a future ruler as the next "Hitler."

Lest someone wonder where this future Gog is actually from, Ezekiel says he will rule over *Magog*, *Meshech*, and *Tubal* (38:2). These areas extended from north of the Black Sea into northeastern Anatolia. Ezekiel also says he will be from "the remote parts of the north" (38:15). His empire will extend from above the Black Sea down into the area between the Black and Caspian Seas.

All the allies of Gog match up with areas that today are either dominated by Islamic fundamentalism or are struggling with it.

Ezekiel says this ruler will also have several allies. He identifies them as *Persia*, *Cush*, and *Put* (38:5). Persia is modern-day Iran, Cush is the region south of Egypt that includes Sudan, and Put was the area west of Egypt—today known as Libya. Ezekiel also lists two other countries in this alliance—*Gomer* and *Beth-togarmah* (38:6). Both groups began in the region around the Black and Caspian Seas and migrated into modern Turkey.

Overlaying these ancient nations and groups on a contemporary map leads to an interesting discovery: all the allies of Gog match up with areas that today are either dominated by Islamic fundamentalism or are struggling with it. Iran became an Islamic state under Ayatollah Khomeini. The northern half of Sudan harbored bin Laden for a time, and the country served as an arms transport base funneling weapons from Iran to Hamas. Libya has disintegrated into warring factions, with some groups supplying fighters and weapons to ISIS and to Islamic forces in Egypt and Gaza. Although Turkey is officially a secular Muslim country, the party in power has its roots in Islamic fundamentalism, and harbors visions of Turkish imperialism and a revived Ottoman Empire.

These countries aren't natural allies, but two factors enable them to overcome their differences: a common hatred for Israel and an overwhelming desire for material gain. The leader from the north will forge together a coalition sharing these mutual interests and goals.

God announces in advance that these invaders will be defeated in a way that demonstrates to Israel that God is in control. "'It will come about on that day, when Gog comes against the land of Israel,' declares the Lord God, 'that My fury will mount up in My anger. In My zeal and in My blazing wrath I declare that on that day there will certainly be a great earthquake in the land of Israel'"

(38:18–19). The ultimate "act of God"—a devastating earthquake at the precise time these invaders reach Israel—stops the armies in their tracks. But God isn't done.

In the confusion caused by the earthquake, "Every man's sword will be against his brother" (38:21). The confusion caused by the earthquake is multiplied by the babble of languages from the different invading forces, leading the panicked allies to begin fighting one another. And yet God still isn't done. "With plague and with blood I will enter into judgment with him; and I will rain on him and on his troops, and on the many peoples who are with him, a torrential rain, hailstones, fire, and brimstone" (v. 22). Plague decimates the troops; hailstones rain down—and because of the earthquake, there is no shelter under which to hide. "Brimstone" might describe a volcanic eruption. The Golan Heights, which are the natural entry point for this northern army, are dotted with extinct volcanoes. God seems to choose this precise moment in time to awaken those mountains from their slumber.

God concludes: "So I will prove Myself great, show Myself holy, and make Myself known in the sight of many nations; and they will know that I am the LORD" (v. 23). The effects of the battle will have international repercussions.

These countries invade at a time when Israel is at peace. This fits well with the first half of the still-future tribulation period, but not the second half. Ezekiel also says one key outcome of the battle is that Israel will come to know her God. At the very beginning of the tribulation Israel makes an agreement with the Antichrist. But by the middle of the seven-year period Israel refuses to accept him as god. It's this battle that marks the change. God uses this invasion—and His destruction of the invaders—to begin turning Israel's heart toward Him in national repentance.

Where is the United States in Bible prophecy?

Though some have tried to find the United States in Bible prophecy, such attempts are doomed to failure. By the end times, the United States ceases to be a major influence in the world. This seems hard to imagine since our country plays such a dominant role in the world today. Yet it is strangely absent in the end-time drama. What could cause its role to diminish so dramatically?

One possibility is that the United States will decline when God removes Christians from the earth just before the beginning of the final seven-year period. Today, as many as half of all Americans claim to be "born again" believers in Jesus Christ. Even if only a relatively small portion of that number have made a genuine personal commitment to Christ, it still means millions of Americans will suddenly "disappear" when God removes His church from the earth. Imagine the effects on the United States if millions of people—in industry, government, the military, business, agriculture, education, medicine, and communications—suddenly vanish! A political and economic collapse will occur when our society suddenly loses those followers of Jesus who were its "salt and light." The chaos will be overwhelming.

A second possibility is that America could become an also-ran society *before* the church is taken from the earth. Our country is undergoing a time of unprecedented social and political upheaval.

In the past God blessed America because it provided the ideal soil for His Word to take root and flourish. Our founding principles included freedom of religion. Missionaries from the United States took the good news of salvation through Jesus Christ to the remotest parts of the world, and with that good news came advances in agriculture, medicine, government, and morality.

A political and economic collapse will occur when our society suddenly loses those followers of Jesus who were its "salt and light."

But today America is in moral decline. When a country ceases to produce fruits of righteousness, it can no longer expect God to bless.

God has also blessed America because of our friendship with the Jewish people and the state of Israel. When God called Abraham, He promised that He would "bless those who bless you, and the one who curses you I will curse" (Gen. 12:3). That principle still holds true. The United States was the first country to recognize the modern state of Israel, and we have been Israel's close ally and supporter for the past eight decades. In recent years, however, a rising number have questioned that support for Israel. Should the United States turn its back on the State of Israel, we will make ourselves an enemy of God. This doesn't mean we always approve of everything Israel does, but we must continue to affirm Israel's right to exist as a Jewish state in the land God has promised to her. If we don't, we could experience God's judgment on our land.

We aren't told why the United States is absent from end-time events, but it's clear that the worldwide center of focus in the end times moves back toward Europe and the Middle East. That is where the final act of God's drama will be played out.

Is China in Bible prophecy?

Two passages in the book of Revelation are said to be possible references to China. The first is Revelation 9:14–16. A voice from the altar before God in heaven speaks "to the sixth angel who had the trumpet, 'Release the four angels who are bound at the great river Euphrates.' And the four angels, who had been prepared for the hour and day and month and year, were released, so that they would kill a third of mankind. The number of the armies of the horsemen was two hundred million; I heard the number of them."

Because of the vast size of this army, some believe China is the only country that would be able to field a force that large. And yet, even though China's army "is the largest standing ground force in the world,"[3] its overall size is just over three million. This is far short of the total number mentioned in Revelation 9.

A second problem is that the passage goes on to describe these "invaders" in a way that makes it more likely they are a demonic force rather than a human army. "And this is how I saw in my vision the horses and those who sat on them: the riders had breastplates the color of fire, of hyacinth, and of brimstone; and the heads of the horses are like the heads of lions; and out of their mouths came fire and smoke and brimstone. A third of mankind was killed by these three plagues, by the fire, the smoke, and the brimstone which came out of their mouths. For the power of the horses is in their mouths and in their tails; for their tails are like serpents and have heads, and with them they do harm" (9:17–19). While some try to find in John's vision an ancient description of modern military equipment, that causes even greater difficulty, because it would require not just two hundred million soldiers but also two hundred million tanks, planes, helicopters, or other military hardware.

Within the context of Revelation 9 this invading force makes more sense if it is a demonic army. When the fifth trumpet is sounded in verses 1–12 a demonic horde with the power to *torment* humanity for five months was released (v. 5). And then when the sixth trumpet sounds, an even greater judgment occurs. Angelic forces release a demonic army that has the power to *kill* a third of the world's population (vv. 15, 18).

The second possible passage linking China to end-time events is found in Revelation 16:12. "The sixth angel poured out his bowl on the great river, the Euphrates; and its water was dried up, so that the way would be prepared for the kings from the east." This event immediately precedes the gathering of the "kings of the entire world" at Armageddon (16:14–16). It's possible that China is included in this gathering of nations, assuming that China hasn't been destroyed up to this point in the tribulation. The passage suggests that all remaining world leaders will move their armies toward Israel for a final climactic battle. But no specific countries, including China, are identified by name.

Does Europe play a role
in Bible prophecy?

Recent history hasn't been kind to Europe or the European Union. Financial crises have exposed a deep-seated rift between the have and have-not countries of Europe. The northern members of the EU have remained relatively strong and prosperous, but the countries in the southern tier have struggled economically. Britain's departure from the EU also impacted the continent's overall stability. Some even wondered if this experiment in European unity, along with the currency it spawned, could survive.[4]

And yet, in spite of the challenges, the EU continues to be an active player in the global economy. The different countries, especially the smaller ones, rely on the EU's central authority, single currency, and unified standards to provide them with a competitive advantage. However, scratch beneath the surface and you still discover problems facing the EU. What's less obvious is that much of this was predicted by the prophet Daniel.

In Daniel 2–7 the prophet describes the period commonly called the "times of the Gentiles"—a time when Gentile powers would rule over the Jewish people, controlling the land of Israel and the city of Jerusalem. In chapters 2 and 7 the prophet focuses on a series of four Gentile powers that will rule Israel from the time of Nebuchadnezzar until the coming of God's kingdom. Chapter 2 pictures the nations as four parts of a giant statue while chapter 7 describes the nations as four beasts climbing out from the sea.

The four empires identified by Daniel are Babylon, Medo-Persia, Greece, and Rome. They form an unbroken line of descent from Daniel's day until the time of Christ. And true to the prediction, Rome was controlling the land at the first coming of the Messiah. But Daniel's prophecy hasn't yet been completely fulfilled.

The final kingdom pictured by Daniel at the conclusion of each vision is *not* the present church age. We don't live in a time when "the sovereignty, the dominion, and the greatness of all the kingdoms under the whole heaven will be given to the people of the saints of the Highest One" (7:27). The messianic kingdom at the end of Daniel's vision is still in the future. And Daniel pictures the fourth Gentile empire continuing until the arrival of God's messianic kingdom. A revised version of the Roman Empire needs to arise in the end times to enable Daniel's prophecies to be fulfilled.

Daniel 9 provides a prophetic timetable that includes a key detail on the reappearance of the fourth Gentile empire. Daniel was told, "The people *of the prince who is to come* will destroy the city and the sanctuary" (9:26, emphasis added). It was the Romans who destroyed Jerusalem and the temple in AD 70. They are the "people of the prince who is to come." This still-future ruler, who is then described in v. 27, is identified through his connection to the nation that destroyed Jerusalem. The one still coming for the final seven years of the tribulation period is connected to the empire that destroyed Jerusalem in AD 70!

Daniel's identification of the Roman Empire's reappearance prior to the return of Christ also aligns with the book of Revelation. In Revelation 13 John describes the end-time empire that will control the earth. He portrays it as "a beast coming up out of the sea" (v. 1), using the same imagery as Daniel 7.

As John continues his verbal portrait, it becomes obvious he is describing the fourth beast of Daniel 7. John's beast has "ten horns and seven heads" (Rev. 13:1) while Daniel said his fourth beast "had ten horns" (Dan. 7:7). Daniel identified the horns on the beast he saw. "As for the ten horns, out of this kingdom ten kings will arise" (Dan. 7:24). John identifies the ten horns on his beast the same way. "The ten horns which you saw are ten kings" (Rev. 17:12). Daniel said this fourth beast will persecute the people of Israel. The saints "will be handed over to him for a time, times, and half a time" (Dan. 7:25). A "time" is symbolic of a year so "a time, times, and half a time" refers to a period of three-and-a-half years. As John describes this end-time evil empire, he says its ruler will be given "authority to act for forty-two months" (Rev. 13:5)—exactly three-and-a-half years.

God provides three clues regarding this final empire that will play a role in end-time events. First, the Antichrist's empire will come from the area once controlled by the Roman Empire. Second, it will include a potent military force. The rest of the world will look at this final world ruler and his empire and say, "Who is able to wage war with him?" (Rev. 13:4). Finally, though the empire will be strong militarily and economically, it will be fractured politically. "And in that you saw the feet and toes, partly of potter's clay and partly of iron, it will be a divided kingdom; but it will have within it some of the toughness of iron, since you saw the iron mixed with common clay" (Dan. 2:41). This revived Roman Empire might be strong militarily, but it will be hampered by each country's continuing sense of nationalism. "In that you saw the iron mixed with common clay, they will combine with one another in their descendants; but they will not adhere to one another, just as iron does not combine with pottery" (v. 43).

Europe—a socially fractured empire possessing military might and an ability to project its power internationally. It will be held together by the sheer force of one man—the one the Bible calls the Antichrist!

17

Who are the 144,000?

The 144,000 are said to be "144,000, sealed from every tribe of the sons of Israel" (Rev. 7:4). Their role appears to be similar to that of Jesus' original disciples—to announce the coming of the Messiah and the kingdom. Beginning in Revelation 7:9 John describes "a great multitude which no one could count, from every nation and all the tribes, peoples, and languages" who apparently come to faith because of the witness of the 144,000.

A careful study of the tribes identified reveals some potential contradictions within the list. For example, the tribe of Dan is left out. The tribe of Ephraim is left out, though the tribe of "Joseph" is probably intended to refer to Ephraim. (Joseph had two sons, Ephraim and Manassesh. Manasseh was the oldest son, but Ephraim became the dominant tribe.) It's likely that Joseph is used here to refer to Ephraim . . . since Manasseh is listed separately. In place of Dan, the tribe of Levi is included. Levi was one of the sons of Jacob, but the tribe of Levi was not given a specific land promise. Instead, the Levites were scattered among the other tribes.

By leaving out Dan and including Levi, the number remained at twelve. Of course, someone might ask why the tribe of Dan would be left out. The text doesn't say, so we need to hold any potential answer loosely. Some suggest that Dan was excluded because of idolatry among the Danites, perhaps represented by the golden calf being set up in Dan. Others suggest the tribe of Dan was excluded because the Danites were the only tribe that deliberately chose to move from the land allotted to them by God and find another place to live (cf. Josh. 19:40–48 and Judg. 18:1–31). There are some who even believe the Antichrist will come from the tribe of Dan. However, there is no biblical evidence at all to back up any of these suggestions.

For whatever reason, God does not select witnesses from the tribe of Dan to be part of His worldwide proclamation during the future tribulation period. But this *doesn't* mean God has completely rejected the tribe of Dan. In Ezekiel 48:1 the tribe of Dan is included in God's future and final allotment of the land among the tribes of Israel. So, there is still a future for this tribe, even though they are not chosen as witnesses during the tribulation.

18

Are the two witnesses predicted in Revelation 11 actually Moses and Elijah?

The two witnesses don't necessarily have to be Moses and Elijah, though their actions sound very similar to these two individuals. Elijah did call fire down from heaven and ask God to withhold rain. And Moses turned water into blood and produced many other plagues. We also know Elijah was taken directly into heaven on a fiery chariot without having to die (2 Kings 2:11) and that Satan disputed with Michael the archangel over the body of Moses (Jude 9). We also know that in Malachi 4 God announced the coming of Elijah. "Behold, I am going to send you Elijah the prophet before the coming of the great and terrible day of the LORD" (v. 5).

However, the problem with requiring Moses and Elijah to physically fulfill the prediction regarding these two witnesses is that Jesus said John the Baptist could have fulfilled the prophecy about Elijah. "And He answered and said, 'Elijah is coming and will restore all things; but I say to you that Elijah already came, and they did not recognize him, but did to him whatever they wanted. So also the Son of Man is going to suffer at their hands.' Then the disciples understood that He had spoken to them about John the Baptist" (Matt. 17:11–13). Earlier in Matthew Jesus told the people, "And if you are willing to accept it, John himself is Elijah who was to come" (11:14). Jesus was saying that John the

Baptist had the potential to fulfill the prophecy regarding Elijah depending on whether or not the people responded properly. And if John the Baptist could have been the fulfillment of the prophecy concerning Elijah, then it would seem that Revelation 11 wouldn't require a literal Moses or a literal Elijah for its fulfillment either.

The key point is to recognize that God will send two prophetic witnesses during the end time, and their ministries will parallel those of Moses and Elijah. But while it's possible that they will be the literal Moses and Elijah returned to earth, that isn't required.

What is the significance of the mark of the beast and the number 666? Are they somehow connected with computer chips, credit cards, and a cashless society?

Three short verses have generated a great deal of controversy: "And he causes all, the small and the great, the rich and the poor, and the free and the slaves, to be given a mark on their right hands or on their foreheads, and he decrees that no one will be able to buy or to sell, except the one who has the mark, either the name of the beast or the number of his name. Here is wisdom. Let him who has understanding calculate the number of the beast, for the number is that of a man; and his number is six hundred and sixty-six" (Rev. 13:16–18). So what is the "mark of the beast"?

It's best to begin with what's most clearly explained in the passage. The "mark of the beast" is either the name of the Antichrist or the "number of his name" that all people will be required to place on their arms or foreheads. The mark is intended as a sign of identification, loyalty, and submission to the Antichrist. It is *not* something a person could receive

When the events in Revelation are being fulfilled, the significance of the number will make perfect sense. Right now, however, it's not clear. That has led to a great deal of unhealthy speculation.

unwittingly. Economic pressure will be applied to get everyone to submit. "No one will be able to buy or to sell, except the one who has the mark" (v. 17).

Though the "mark" is said to be either the name of the Antichrist or the number of his name (666), it is not explained in any greater detail. When the events in Revelation are being fulfilled, the significance of the number will make perfect sense. Right now, however, it's not clear. That has led to a great deal of unhealthy speculation. Many people have offered guesses regarding the identity of the Antichrist or the interpretation of the number . . . like a security code or chip on a credit card, a tattoo, or a universal ID. When it comes to interpreting prophecy, it can always be helpful at such times simply to say, "I don't know, but it will make perfect sense at the proper time."

What we *do* know is that this mark of allegiance is not something an individual could receive accidentally. The passage says everyone will be forced to receive the mark in order to be able to buy or sell. People will know when they are getting it.

20

What is the Battle of Armageddon?
Is it the end of the world?

The Bible never actually describes a "battle" of Armageddon. Revelation 16:16 says the Antichrist, Satan, and the false prophet send out demons, and "they gathered them together to the place which in Hebrew is called Har-Magedon." It seems more accurate to describe this gathering as the beginning of the *campaign* of Armageddon.

Armageddon, which is a transliteration of the Hebrew words *har Megiddo* ("hill of Megiddo"), is the ideal staging area for the Antichrist and his army. Megiddo looks out over the strategic Jezreel Valley that cuts through Israel from the Mediterranean to the Jordan River. Ships can come from the west and dock at Haifa. The ancient International Highway connecting Egypt and Mesopotamia runs through the Jezreel Valley very near Megiddo. Before the Antichrist's final campaign begins, he needs to gather and prepare his armies. Armageddon becomes that staging place.

The Bible never actually describes a "battle" of Armageddon.

The final "battle" itself, recorded in Revelation 19, takes place when Christ returns to earth. Verse 19 says, "And I saw the beast and the kings of the earth and their armies, assembled to make war against Him who sat on the horse, and against His army." The gap between the gathering of the armies (Rev. 16) and the actual battle (Rev. 19) allows for other events to take place. Four different scriptures suggest the final, climactic battle will take place in Jerusalem.

Joel 3:9–16 describes the end times when nations will beat their plowshares into swords and "come up to the Valley of Jehoshaphat" where God will "judge all the surrounding nations" (v. 12). Some believe the Valley of Jehoshaphat refers either to the Kidron or Hinnom Valleys on the edge of Jerusalem. Others think it might refer to the valley formed when the Mount of Olives splits in two in Zechariah 14:4–5. In either case, the judgment of the invading nations takes place at Jerusalem. In Joel 2:32 and 3:16 God specifically says His deliverance comes to "Mount Zion" and "Jerusalem."

Daniel 11:36–45 describes the final campaign of the Antichrist. As part of his final campaign he "will also enter the Beautiful Land" (v. 41). This could be the initial "gathering" of his armies at Armageddon. He then invades North Africa (vv. 42–43), before pivoting in response to a threat "from the East and from the North" (v. 44). This could possibly parallel the destruction of Babylon described in Revelation 17–18. Finally, the Antichrist will "pitch the tents of his royal pavilion between the seas and the beautiful Holy Mountain" (v. 45). The "seas" refer to the Mediterranean Sea and the Dead Sea, and the "beautiful Holy Mountain" is Mount Zion or the Temple Mount. That's where the Antichrist "will come to his end, and no one will help him" (v. 45b). Daniel specifically places the final battle and defeat of the Antichrist at Jerusalem.

Zechariah 12:8–10 reveals God's vow "to destroy all the nations that come against Jerusalem" (v. 9). He also promises to deliver the Jewish people when they "look at Me whom they pierced" (v. 10). Jesus' return takes place as the armies are fighting in Jerusalem.

Zechariah 14:2–5, 12 describes a time when God will "gather all the nations against Jerusalem to battle" (v. 2). He then promises to "go forth and fight against those nations, as when He fights on a day of battle. On that day His feet will stand on the Mount of Olives, which is in front of Jerusalem on the east; and the Mount of Olives will be split in its middle from east to west forming a very large valley. Half of the mountain will move toward the north, and the other half toward the south" (vv. 3–4). God specifically vows to "strike all the peoples who have gone to war against Jerusalem" (v. 12).

Rather than being the end of the world, the campaign that begins at Armageddon ends with Jesus returning to earth as King of kings and Lord of lords to defeat His foes and usher in His millennial kingdom.

Do the Jewish festivals point to the time of Christ's return?

Israel's festivals are prophetically significant. God designed them to point both to the first coming and second coming of the Messiah.

The spring feasts pointed toward Jesus' first coming:

- **Passover**—Jesus was the ultimate Passover lamb who died for the sins of the world (1 Cor. 5:7).
- **Unleavened bread**—Jesus was the sinless one broken for us (1 Cor. 11:23–24).
- **Firstfruits**—Jesus was the firstfruits from the dead (1 Cor. 15:20–23).
- **Shavuot/Pentecost**—Jesus' death and resurrection are the basis for the new covenant blessing, including forgiveness of sin and the outpouring of the Holy Spirit (Acts 2:16–17; 1 Cor. 11:25).

The fall feasts point toward Jesus' second coming:

- **Rosh Hashanah/Feast of Trumpets**—Jesus will return for His bride "at the last trumpet" (1 Cor. 15:52; 1 Thess. 4:16) and God will begin His final days of awe, focusing again in a unique way on Israel.

- **Yom Kippur/Day of Atonement**—Israel "will look at Me whom they pierced; and they will mourn for Him" (Zech. 12:10). As a result, "On that day a fountain will be opened for the house of David and for the inhabitants of Jerusalem, for sin and for defilement" (Zech. 13:1).
- **Sukkot/Feast of Tabernacles**—Israel will experience the joy of being ingathered as a nation, and the nations will join Israel in worshiping the Lord (Zech. 14:16–19).

The spring feasts not only pointed prophetically to Christ, they were also fulfilled on the exact date of the Hebrew calendar. Does this mean the fall feasts (pointing to still-future events) will also be fulfilled on those specific days? While that could be possible, we can't say so with any degree of certainty for at least two reasons. First, Jesus said specifically regarding His second coming, "But about that day and hour no one knows" (Matt. 24:36). If His return were to happen on the exact day of Yom Kippur, it seems people *could* calculate the date with relative precision. Second, the Bible says the future Antichrist will "intend to make alterations in times and in law" (Dan. 7:25), perhaps to sow confusion or to stop the Jewish people from practicing their faith. In either case, it seems unwise to assume these future events will happen on those exact days.

Why will Jesus reign on earth
for a thousand years?

There seem to be at least two reasons Jesus will reign on earth for a thousand years. The first is to allow for the fulfillment of God's Old Testament promises to Israel. For example, in Jeremiah 30:3 God announced He would bring both "Israel and Judah" back from captivity and restore them to the land. He also promised to restore them spiritually so they "shall serve the LORD their God and David their king, whom I will raise up for them" (30:9). God promised to establish His new covenant "with the house of Israel and the house of Judah" (31:31), and in the same chapter He announced Jerusalem would be completely restored. The city "will not be uprooted or overthrown ever again" (v. 40).

These and many other Old Testament promises for Israel have yet to be fulfilled. Micah the prophet ends his book by announcing that a day will come when Israel will be restored and blessed (Mic. 7:11–14). In the very last verse of his book Micah explains why this has to take place. "You will give truth to Jacob and favor to Abraham, *which You swore to our forefathers from the days of old*" (7:20, emphasis added). God made solemn covenant promises to the patriarchs, and Micah said they will come to pass because God is a God who keeps His word. The Old Testament didn't announce the specific length of God's promised kingdom, but the prophets clearly predicted that such a kingdom would come.

There is also a second, more theological, reason for the millennium kingdom. Humanity has always sought an excuse to

WHAT DOES THE BIBLE SAY ABOUT THE FUTURE?

justify its sinful rebellion. "It's the circumstances—or environment—in which we grew up." "It's the poverty and hunger we've faced." "We succumbed to peer pressure." "The devil made us do it." These and other excuses always seek to lay the blame for our sins somewhere else. But in the millennial kingdom God will set up the equivalent of heaven on earth for a thousand years.

Satan will be banished to the abyss. "And he took hold of the dragon, the serpent of old, who is the devil and Satan, and bound him for a thousand years; and he threw him into the abyss and shut it and sealed it over him, so that he would not deceive the nations any longer, until the thousand years were completed" (Rev. 20:2–3). There will be *no satanic influence* during this period.

Jesus will rule in perfect righteousness. "And He will judge between the nations, and will mediate for many peoples; and they will beat their swords into plowshares, and their spears into pruning knives. Nation will not lift up a sword against nation, and never again will they learn war" (Isa. 2:4). There will be *no injustice*.

People born during this thousand-year period will not know poverty, injustice, or oppression.

Everyone will experience universal peace and prosperity. Even animals will be at peace. "And the wolf will dwell with the lamb, and the leopard will lie down with the young goat, and the calf and the young lion and the fattened steer will be together; and a little boy will lead them" (Isa. 11:6). Amos describes the kingdom as a time when people will struggle to harvest all the crops before it's time to plant again. "'Behold, days are coming,' declares the LORD, 'when the plowman will overtake the reaper, and the one who treads grapes will overtake him who sows the seed; when the mountains will drip grape juice, and all the hills will come apart. I will also restore the fortunes of My people Israel, and they will rebuild the desolated cities and live in them; they will also plant vineyards and drink their wine, and make gardens and eat their fruit'" (Amos 9:13–14). There will be *no poverty*.

People born during this thousand-year period will not know poverty, injustice, or oppression. Yet at the end of the thousand years, Satan is given one final opportunity to encourage people to turn against God. "When the thousand years are completed, Satan will be released from his prison, and will come out to deceive the nations" (Rev. 20:7–8). Sadly, Satan will find *many* willing to follow him.

This second purpose for the millennial kingdom is to show that the ultimate problem with humanity has always been our own depravity and sinful nature. It's no accident that immediately following this final rebellion the apostle John describes the great white throne judgment (Rev. 20:11–15). God can righteously judge humanity because He has now demonstrated that the underlying problem has never been external influences—it has *always* been the human heart.

23

Will everyone in the millennium be born again and have glorified bodies? And if so, how can children be born?

When Jesus returns to earth at the end of the tribulation period, there will be both believers and unbelievers still living on earth in their physical bodies. Matthew 25 describes what will happen next. "But when the Son of Man comes in His glory, and all the angels with Him, then He will sit on His glorious throne. And all the nations will be gathered before Him; and He will separate them from one another, just as the shepherd separates the sheep from the goats" (vv. 31–32). Jesus will separate those who are believers from those who are unbelievers. He will say to the believers, "Come, you who are blessed of My Father, inherit the kingdom prepared for you from the foundation of the world" (v. 34). Jesus then says to the unbelievers, "Depart from Me, you accursed people, into the eternal fire which has been prepared for the devil and his angels" (v. 41).

The specific people in focus in these verses are Gentiles. God will be able to determine their spiritual condition based on how they treated the Jewish people during the tribulation. Only true believers will be willing to risk their lives to help the Jews being persecuted. Jesus makes a clear distinction between these two groups, and only those who are saved will be allowed to enter the kingdom.

A similar time of judgment will occur for Jews at the end of the tribulation period. Ezekiel pictures it as a time when all Jews will be gathered and required to pass under the rod of the Great Shepherd. "I will bring you out from the peoples and gather you from the lands where you are scattered, with a mighty hand and with an outstretched arm and with wrath poured out; and I will bring you into the wilderness of the peoples, and there I will enter into judgment with you face to face. . . . I will make you pass under the rod, and I will bring you into the bond of the covenant; and I will purge from you the rebels and those who revolt against Me; I will bring them out of the land where they reside, but they will not enter the land of Israel. So you will know that I am the LORD" (Ezek. 20:34–35, 37–38). Only those Jews who have submitted to the Lord in faith will be allowed to enter the kingdom. This matches Jesus' words to Nicodemus in John 3:3. "Truly, truly, I say to you, unless someone is born again he cannot see the kingdom of God."

When the kingdom begins, all born-again believers who survived the tribulation will be in their natural bodies. However, all Old Testament saints, church-age believers, and those who were martyred during the tribulation will be in the millennial kingdom in resurrected, glorified bodies. Daniel 12:2 and Revelation 20:4 describe the resurrection of the Old Testament and tribulation saints. The resurrection of the church-age saints is pictured in 1 Thessalonians 4:13–18. During the millennium, those in natural bodies will be able to marry and have children, while those in resurrected bodies will not. "For in the resurrection they neither marry nor are given in marriage, but are like angels in heaven" (Matt. 22:30).

Once the millennial kingdom begins, children *will* be born to those who entered the kingdom in natural bodies. This means those children will need to come to faith. Sadly, many will refuse to put their trust in Jesus. That's why, in Revelation 20:7–9, there will be a host of people at the end of the thousand-year period who will join in a final rebellion against Christ. These will be people born during the kingdom age but who refused to trust Jesus.

24

Will animal sacrifices be offered during the millennium? How do we reconcile this with the once-for-all death of Jesus on the cross?

We need to start by recognizing that animal sacrifices *never* took away sin, even in the Old Testament. Hebrews 10:4 says it was "impossible for the blood of bulls and goats to take away sins." The death of God's Son is the only acceptable sacrifice for sin in any age . . . past, present, or future.

In the Old Testament, sacrifices and the annual festivals were intended to look *forward* to the death of Christ. So when Jesus arrived on scene, John the Baptist could call Him "the Lamb of God who takes away the sin of the world!" (John 1:29).

Following Christ's death and resurrection God instituted Communion, or the Lord's Supper. It serves a similar purpose to Old Testament sacrifices in the sense of enabling worshipers to look *back* to the death of Christ. In 1 Corinthians 11:26 Paul says that whenever believers eat the bread and drink from the cup, they "proclaim the Lord's death until He comes." This suggests the ordinance of Communion will cease once the Lord returns to earth.

People born during the future millennial kingdom will still need some type of reminder of what Jesus did for

It will be possible for someone born during the millennium to live his or her entire life and never see something die.

them on the cross. One key reason is that death will be much less frequent during that time. Isaiah described it as a time when "the wolf will dwell with the lamb, and the leopard will lie down with the young goat, and the calf and the young lion and the fattened steer will be together; and a little boy will lead them. Also the cow and the bear will graze, their young will lie down together, and the lion will eat straw like the ox. The nursing child will play by the hole of the cobra, and the weaned child will put his hand on the viper's den. They will not hurt or destroy in all My holy mountain" (Isa. 11:6–9). Isaiah also said it would be a day when "the youth will die at the age of a hundred, and the one who does not reach the age of a hundred will be thought accursed. . . . For as the lifetime of a tree, so will be the days of My people" (65:20, 22). In other words, it will be possible for someone born during the millennium to live his or her entire life and never see something die.

How do you explain the death of Christ to such an individual? Perhaps sacrifices will be reinstituted to look *back* to the death of Christ and serve as a graphic reminder of what Jesus did for them.

One final point. Sacrifices by themselves are not incompatible with the death of Christ. When Paul was arrested in the temple in Acts 21, he was there to pay the expenses for Jewish believers who were completing their Nazirite vows, which included offering animal sacrifices (Acts 21:21–27; Num. 6:13–20). The fact that Paul was in the temple to pay for their sacrifices suggests he didn't see any contradiction between the death of Jesus on the cross and the offering of those animal sacrifices.

25

Why does the tree of life reappear in the book of Revelation?

We need to begin by understanding what the tree of life represented in the Bible. In Genesis 3:22 the reason God banished Adam and Eve from the garden was to deny them access to the tree of life. "He might reach out with his hand, and take fruit also from the tree of life, and eat, and live forever." In Revelation 2:7 God made a promise to the overcomers from the church of Ephesus. "To the one who overcomes, I will grant to eat from the tree of life, which is in the Paradise of God." Presumably, this was intended as a promise that they will live forever.

In Revelation 22:1–3 the tree of life reappears in the New Jerusalem. It's nourished by the water of life flowing from the throne of God. Revelation says the leaves on the tree of life in the New Jerusalem are for the "healing of the nations." But if the New Jerusalem is part of eternity, why would people in perfect, glorified bodies need to be "healed"? To answer that question we need to understand the meaning of the Greek word for healing that John uses. The word is *therapeian* from which we get the word *therapeutic*. We think of *therapeutic* in terms of medical treatment, but the word also had the idea of nurturing, taking care of, attending to, or restoring someone or something. In fact, in Luke 12:42 the word *therapeian* is actually translated "servants."

By using this word God is illustrating the reality that eternal life isn't just measured in the number of days we live, but in the quality of those days as well. The leaves will promote the enjoyment of life, benefiting everyone through all the blessings God will provide. This is made clear by the next verse, which says, "There will no longer be any curse" (Rev. 22:3). The curse of disease and death that came at the time of the fall will be eliminated.

Perhaps the question we ought to ask is this: Why was the tree of life, along with the tree of the knowledge of good and evil, originally placed in the garden of Eden? The Bible doesn't provide an explicit answer, so we need to be careful not to be too dogmatic. But we do know that in the garden of Eden, God provided humanity with both an opportunity for eternal life and an opportunity to gain knowledge of good and evil through obeying Him. God had already announced that the consequence for disobedience would be death.

When Adam and Eve were expelled from the garden, they lost access to the tree of life—until God sent His Son to provide eternal life. Having the tree of life in the garden of Eden suggests that God's gracious plan was always to provide eternal life. And someday His original plan will be realized in the new heavens and new earth. That is why the tree of life reappears in the New Jerusalem.

Is the New Jerusalem
the same as heaven?

The New Jerusalem is the eternal abode of the righteous. The writer of Hebrews says Abraham "was looking for the city which has foundations, whose architect and builder is God" (11:10). A few verses later the writer says God prepared this heavenly "city" for His people (verse 16). In Hebrews 12:22 the city is described as the "city of the living God" and as "the heavenly Jerusalem." This city will be inhabited by "myriads of angels," the "church of the firstborn," "God, the Judge of all," the "spirits of the righteous made perfect," and "Jesus the mediator of a new covenant" (12:22–24). Our eternal abode—along with God, angels, and the redeemed of all ages—will be the heavenly city of Jerusalem!

When most people talk about "heaven" they are referring to the abode of God. Jesus said He was going "to the Father" (John 14:28), and He also said that in the "Father's house are many rooms" (14:2). The apostle Paul said that to be absent from our physical body is to be "at home with the Lord" (2 Cor. 5:8). If heaven is where God dwells, then the New Jerusalem and heaven must both refer to the same place since God is said to dwell in the New Jerusalem. John affirms this in Revelation 21:2–3. "And I saw the holy city, new Jerusalem, coming down out of heaven from God, prepared as a bride adorned for her husband. And I heard a loud voice from the throne, saying, 'Behold, the tabernacle of God is among the people, and He will dwell among them, and they shall be His people, and God Himself will be among them.'"

The dimensions of the New Jerusalem are given in Revelation 21:16. It's said to be "twelve thousand stadia" (just under one thousand four hundred miles) long, wide, and high. We're not told if the shape is a cube or a pyramid, but in either case, it's massive. If we were to stretch a line that long across the United States, it would extend from Chicago to Phoenix, or from Houston to New York City. And a city standing nearly one thousand four hundred miles high is simply beyond our ability to comprehend.

> **The first heaven is the atmosphere around us, and the second heaven includes all of outer space. The third heaven exists outside the known universe and is the very presence of God.**

In 2 Corinthians 12:2 Paul describes a time when he was "caught up to the third heaven." The first heaven is the atmosphere around us, and the second heaven includes all of outer space. The third heaven exists outside the known universe and is the very presence of God. Two verses later Paul says he was "caught up into Paradise" (v. 4). So Paradise is another name for the third heaven, this abode of God. Jesus said to the thief on the cross, "Truly I say to you, today you will be with Me in Paradise" (Luke 23:43). Since Jesus said He was going "to the Father" in John 14:28, we know that Paradise must be still another name for the New Jerusalem or heaven.

Who will be judged at the great white throne judgment?

At the great white throne judgment in Revelation 20 God judges all the unsaved of all ages. The judgment begins with "the dead, the great and the small, standing before the throne" (v. 12). Two books are opened. The first is a set of books that record what each person had done in life. "The dead were judged from the things which were written in the books, according to their deeds" (v. 12). Sadly, this list of deeds each has committed is sufficient to condemn him or her to the lake of fire for all eternity. This place of judgment is referred to as "the second death" (vv. 14–15).

God also opens a second book, described as "the book of life" (v. 12). This book records the names of all who have been redeemed. In Psalm 69:28 David connects the "book of life" to those who have been declared "righteous." In Philippians 4:3 Paul describes his fellow workers as those "whose names are in the book of life." Revelation 13:8 adds one additional characteristic of this book. It is "the book of life of the Lamb who has been slaughtered." Those whose names are in the book of life belong to Jesus because of His redemptive work.

As the deeds of each unredeemed individual are laid bare before almighty God, it becomes clear that the offenses are sufficient to condemn each one to the lake of fire. In one of the saddest verses of the Bible, John writes, "And if anyone's name was not found written in the book of life, he was thrown into the lake of fire" (Rev. 20:15). With the exception of Jesus, everyone who has ever lived has sinned and deserves God's judgment. The one item that will make an eternal difference is whether or not a person's name has been recorded in the book of life.

> **Faith alone in Christ alone is what gets someone's name written in the Lamb's book of life.**

Thankfully, believers don't appear before God at the great white throne judgment. In 1 John 5:12–13 John writes, "The one who has the Son has the life; the one who does not have the Son of God does not have the life. These things I have written to you who believe in the name of the Son of God, so that you may know that you have eternal life." Faith alone in Christ alone is what gets someone's name written in the Lamb's book of life.

Though Christians will not appear at the great white throne judgment, Christians *will* appear before God's *bema* seat for judgment. In 2 Corinthians 5:10 Paul says church-age believers "must all appear before the judgment seat [*bema*] of Christ, so that each one may receive compensation for his deeds done through the body, in accordance with what he has done, whether good or bad." For believers, what's at stake in this judgment is not a loss of salvation, but a loss of reward. There are levels of reward in eternity that believers will experience. In 1 Corinthians 3 Paul talks about the quality of the works done by believers. Some are "gold, silver, precious stones" while others are "wood, hay, or straw" (v. 12). Paul then describes the results of this judgment, when all these works will be revealed and tested. "If anyone's work which he has built on it remains, he will receive a reward. If anyone's work is burned up, he will suffer loss; but he himself will be saved, *yet only so as through fire*" (vv. 14–15, emphasis added). Both groups are in heaven, but one group is there without the eternal rewards experienced by others.

The Bible is consistent in saying that our eternal destiny is based on what Jesus did for us on the cross, not on what we do for ourselves. What we possess in the kingdom might vary, but all who have put their trust in Christ *will* be in the kingdom.

What is the purpose for Bible prophecy? Why did God predict the future?

God shared predictions about the future for at least three reasons. First, such predictions validate God's claims regarding His character and His power. By announcing events in advance and then causing them to happen, God demonstrated His absolute authority and control over the universe. In Isaiah 41–48 God repeatedly uses His ability to announce what the future holds to show His superiority to any other supposed god.

- "I am the LORD, that is My name; I will not give My glory to another, nor My praise to idols. Behold, the former things have come to pass, now I declare new things; before they sprout I proclaim them to you" (Isa. 42:8–9).
- "Who among them can declare this and proclaim to us the former things? Let them present their witnesses so that they may be justified, or let them hear and say, 'It is true.' 'You are My witnesses,' declares the LORD, 'and My servant whom I have chosen, so that you may know and believe Me and understand that I am He. Before Me there was no God formed, and there will be none after Me. I, only I, am the LORD, and there is no savior besides Me'" (Isa. 43:9–11).
- "This is what the LORD says, He who is the King of Israel and his Redeemer, the LORD of armies: 'I am the first and I am

the last, and there is no God besides Me. Who is like Me? Let him proclaim and declare it; and, let him confront Me beginning with My establishing of the ancient nation. Then let them declare to them the things that are coming and the events that are going to take place'" (Isa. 44:6–7).

- "Gather yourselves and come; come together, you survivors of the nations! They have no knowledge, who carry around their wooden idol and pray to a god who cannot save. Declare and present your case; indeed, let them consult together. Who has announced this long ago? Who has long since declared it? Is it not I, the LORD? And there is no other God besides Me, a righteous God and a Savior; there is none except Me" (Isa. 45:20–21).

- "Remember the former things long past, for I am God, and there is no other; I am God, and there is no one like Me, declaring the end from the beginning, and from ancient times things which have not been done, saying, 'My plan will be established, and I will accomplish all My good pleasure'" (Isa. 46:9–10).

- "I declared the former things long ago, and they went out of My mouth, and I proclaimed them. Suddenly I acted, and they came to pass. Because I know that you are obstinate, and your neck is an iron tendon and your forehead bronze, therefore I declared them to you long ago, before they took place I proclaimed them to you. . . . For My own sake, for My own sake, I will act; for how can My name be profaned? And I will not give My glory to another" (Isa. 48:3–5, 11).

Isaiah recorded these words around 700 BC after God had announced that Judah would be taken into captivity in Babylon

(Isa. 39:5–7), but beginning in chapter 40 God promises to restore His people from that still-future captivity. And as if to punctuate the reality that He is in control of time itself, God provides a dramatic prediction. In the center of all these statements about His unique power God makes the following announcement. "This is what the LORD says *to Cyrus* His anointed, whom I have taken by the right hand, to subdue nations before him and to undo the weapons belt on the waist of kings; to open doors before him so that gates will not be shut. . . . For the sake of Jacob My servant, and Israel My chosen one, *I have also called you by your name*; I have given you a title of honor though you have not known Me" (45:1, 4, emphasis added).

God identified the ruler who would defeat Babylon and issue a command to allow the Jewish people to return home. And He made that specific announcement 170 years before the event happened! How significant is this? It would be comparable to having George Washington announce at his inauguration in 1789 that another American military commander named Dwight Eisenhower would become the thirty-fourth president. From a human perspective such a prediction is impossible. And that's God's point. Only He can make such a dramatic announcement because He alone is God and in control of history even before it occurs.

The second reason God predicted the future was to validate both His messenger and His message. This is especially true concerning the person and work of His Son. How could Israel know when their Messiah had arrived? They could look for someone who would:

- Be born of a virgin (Isa. 7:14)
- Be born in Bethlehem (Mic. 5:2)

- Receive gold and frankincense from kings who would come to worship Him (Isa. 60:1–6)
- Perform miracles of healing on the blind, deaf, lame, and mute (Isa. 35:4–6)
- Ride into Jerusalem on the exact day predicted by Daniel (Dan. 9:25)
- Ride into Jerusalem on a colt, the foal of a donkey (Zech. 9:9)

And these are just *some* of the predictions about the Messiah that validated Jesus' claims!

But there's a third reason God prophesied the future. He pulled back the curtain of time and revealed the future to give His followers hope and comfort. Knowing what the Bible says about the future helps God's followers place life's events in their proper perspective. God reveals His plans and purposes to enable us to walk by faith rather than live in fear. Paul began his prediction of the rapture (1 Thess. 4:13–18) by saying he didn't want believers "to be uninformed . . . about those who are asleep, so that you will not grieve as indeed the rest of mankind do, who have no hope" (v. 13). Paul then ends his description of these events with a reassuring message of hope. "Therefore, comfort one another with these words" (v. 18).

[God] pulled back the curtain of time and revealed the future to give His followers hope and comfort.

God gave prophecy to produce stability and holy living. In 2 Peter 3 the apostle describes the coming of scoffers who deny the reality of God's predictions regarding the future. Peter reminds them of God's patience, but he also affirms the reality that the final "day of judgment and destruction" (v. 7) is coming. Then, having explained what the future holds, Peter shares a very practical application of how that truth should impact our lives today. "Since all these things are to be destroyed in this way, what sort of people ought you to be in holy conduct and godliness, looking for and hastening the coming of the day of God, because of which the heavens will be destroyed by burning, and the elements will melt with intense heat! But according to His promise we are looking for new heavens and a new earth, in which righteousness dwells. Therefore, beloved, since you look for these things, be diligent to be found spotless and blameless by Him, at peace" (v. 11–14).

Prophecy gives God's followers hope, comfort, and stability in what could otherwise be turbulent times!

Why did God tell us about some events in the future but not others?

God provided enough information regarding the future to give His followers confidence in His power and control, and to keep them from being deceived by false prophets and false teaching. When Jesus gave His disciples details about the tribulation period in Matthew 24, He paused at one point to share why this truth is so important. "Then if anyone says to you, 'Behold, here is the Christ,' or 'He is over here,' do not believe him. For false christs and false prophets will arise and will provide great signs and wonders, so as to mislead, if possible, even the elect. Behold, *I have told you in advance*" (vv. 23–25, emphasis added).

Peter offered a similar reminder both at the beginning and at the end of his second epistle. He first reminded his readers that "we have the prophetic word made more sure, to which you do well to pay attention as to a lamp shining in a dark place" (1:19). Prophecy helps shine a light on events swirling around us that can otherwise seem very confusing. Peter ended his letter by again reminding his readers of the importance of focusing on what God had predicted in His Word. "You therefore, beloved, knowing this beforehand, be on your guard so that you **When it comes to prophecy we need to focus on the big picture.** are not carried away by the error of unscrupulous people and lose your own firm commitment" (3:17).

So why didn't God share more details about the future?

One reason God didn't tell us more about the future is that the sheer volume of material would lead to information overload. Possessing too much information can actually make it more difficult for an individual to understand and process everything. God focused on the major milestones lest we become distracted by a myriad of details. And that serves as a good reminder: when it comes to prophecy we need to focus on the big picture.

Another reason God didn't tell us more about the future is that He wants to make sure we learn to walk by faith. In the middle of describing the reality of our future presence with the Lord, Paul paused to share a practical reminder of life this side of heaven, where "we walk by faith, not by sight" (2 Cor. 5:7). The word "walk" has the idea in that passage of making our way through life. God didn't share all the details of what the future holds because He wants us to learn how to depend on Him each step of the way.

Jesus encouraged the same perspective on the future in His Sermon on the Mount. He told the multitude, "But seek first His kingdom and His righteousness, and all these things will be provided to you. So do not worry about tomorrow; for tomorrow will worry about itself. Each day has enough trouble of its own" (Matt. 6:33–34). If we focus on God and His coming kingdom, we can trust Him to work out the other details of our lives.

30

If prophecy is true, what difference should it make in my life today?

God gave some of the most dramatic and extensive predictions of future events to the apostle John in the book of Revelation. But having described the future, John returns to the present at the end of the final chapter. His closing words focus on the impact that the future ought to have on our lives today. John first drives home the fact that everything he has described will happen just as God predicted. "And he said to me, 'These words are faithful and true'; and the Lord, the God of the spirits of the prophets, sent His angel to show His bond-servants the things which must soon take place" (22:6). Jesus then added His testimony to that of the angel. "And behold, I am coming quickly. Blessed is the one who keeps the words of the prophecy of this book" (v. 7).

God's predictions regarding the future *will* come to pass. Christ *will* return. Everything God has announced *will* take place. But how do you align with God's program for the future? When Christ returns in the air for His church, will He take you with Him to heaven? Do you know without a doubt that heaven is your eternal destiny?

Help for those who aren't sure

After describing the beauty of the New Jerusalem, John offers his audience an opportunity to respond. He first turns to those who are not sure of their eternal destiny, who don't know if they will be with Jesus in the New Jerusalem. John offers a message of hope to these readers. "The Spirit [the Holy Spirit] and the bride [the New Jerusalem] say, 'Come.' And let the one who hears say, 'Come.' And let the one who is thirsty come; let the one who desires, take the water of life without cost" (22:17).

Have you ever responded to God in this way? We have all done wrong and broken God's commands. In the book of Romans Paul reminds us that "all have sinned and fall short of the glory of God" (3:23). Because everyone does wrong things, we assume God will somehow "grade on the curve" and lower His entrance requirements for heaven. But God never lowers His standards. "For the wages of sin is death" (6:23). Only someone who is absolutely perfect (like Jesus Christ) can ever be good enough to get into heaven through his own ability.

God wants us to be with Him for eternity. But we have sinned, and our sin must be punished. Thankfully, God provided a way to pay for our sin so we can spend eternity with Him. "But God demonstrates His own love toward us, in that while we were still sinners, Christ died for us" (5:8). Jesus was the perfect God/man. He lived a perfect life, and then He died on the cross to take on Himself the punishment for our wrongdoings. God's Son paid the penalty for our sin, and now He is standing and holding out eternal life to you as a gift. That's why the Spirit and the bride say, "Come!" God has already paid the price to purchase eternal life for you. All you need to do is "take the free gift of the water of life."

How can you receive eternal life today? Acknowledge to God that you have sinned and that you can't get into heaven by your good efforts. Believe that Jesus Christ, God's eternal Son, became a man and died on the cross to pay for your sins. The fact that He rose from the dead proves that His payment was sufficient. Then place your trust in Jesus Christ for your eternal destiny. You can do this right now by praying a simple prayer like the following:

> Dear Lord, I know that I have done wrong and fallen short of Your perfect ways. I realize that my sins have separated me from You. I believe that You sent Your Son, Jesus Christ, to earth to die on the cross for my sins. I put my trust in Jesus Christ and what He did on the cross as payment for my sins. Please forgive me and give me eternal life. Amen.

If you just prayed that prayer in sincerity, welcome to the family of God! God has promised that all who put their trust in Jesus Christ as their Savior will receive eternal life. "For God so loved the world, that He gave His only Son, so that everyone who believes in Him will not perish, but have eternal life" (John 3:16). And as you learned in this book, you can count on God to keep His promise!

Here are some final suggestions. Begin reading your Bible. Start in the New Testament in the gospel of John to read more about the One who died to pay for your sins. Try to find a good church in your area where they believe and teach the Bible. A church is not a gathering place for perfect people. It is more like a hospital where hurting people can go to be mended spiritually. Tell the pastor of your decision to accept Christ, and ask him for guidance to help you grow as a Christian.

Hope for those who are sure

After explaining to his readers how prophecy relates to those who have not yet put their trust in Christ, John ends the book of Revelation by sharing with those who have trusted in Christ. How should the great truths of Bible prophecy influence believers? John provides the answer in Revelation 22:20. "He who testifies to these things [and he's referring to Jesus] says, 'Yes, I am coming quickly.'" Believers must remember that Jesus Christ *is* coming back to take them to be with Him in heaven. This is the *next* event on God's prophetic calendar.

Christ reminds those who have put their trust in Him that He could come back at any time. John then speaks the words that should be on the lips of everyone who has placed his or her trust in Christ. "Amen. Come, Lord Jesus." God's words of prophecy force us to shift our gaze away from our problems in life and look toward heaven. As difficult as life might seem right now, it will not remain so forever. At any time, Christ could sound His trumpet and come to take us from this world of trouble to spend eternity with Him.

Or, to echo along with John: Amen! Come, Lord Jesus!

Acknowledgments

A book might have a single author's name on the cover, but many people are involved in its writing and printing. The danger in acknowledging some is that I might accidentally leave out others, so I apologize in advance for any omissions. But I can't finish this manuscript without singling out the following individuals to whom I'm especially grateful.

Thank you, Dan Craig, for challenging me to gather some of the questions on prophecy that have been asked on *The Land and the Book* radio program and put them in book form. This project came about because of your prompting!

Thank you, Jon Gauger and Dan Anderson, for your partnership in *The Land and the Book*. It's hard to believe we have been working together for over a decade. I have enjoyed every minute of that time together. This book is just a small slice of the more than two thousand questions we have covered during that time.

A special thank-you to those who have written in to *The Land and the Book* with your questions. As I've said so often on the program, asking questions of a teacher is like saying "Sic 'em!" to a dog. You have motivated me to dig deep and stay sharp!

Thank you, Amy Simpson, for championing my manuscript at Moody Publishers. You and a host of others have worked behind the scenes to turn a digital file into a book that can hopefully make a difference in people's lives.

I end by thanking my wife, Kathy. Those who really know me understand the role Kathy plays in every book I write. She is the in-house editor and proofreader who always makes my initial manuscript look polished and professional. I love you and appreciate all you have done for me over the years!

Notes

1. For a more detailed explanation of this position, see Asher Kaufman, *The Temple Mount: Where Is the Holy of Holies?* (Jerusalem: Har Year'ah Press, 2004). Thomas Ice and Randall Price evaluate this and other suggestions in *Ready to Rebuild: The Imminent Plan to Rebuild the Last Days Temple* (Eugene, OR: Harvest House Publishers, 1972), 154–70.
2. Josephus, *Wars of the Jews* 5.5.5, trans. William Whiston, emphasis added.
3. "Military and Security Developments Involving the People's Republic of China," Department of Defense Annual Report to Congress, 2020, vii.
4. Stefan Lehne, "How the EU Can Survive in a Geopolitical Age," Carnegie Endowment for International Peace, February 25, 2020, https://carnegieeurope.eu/2020/02/25/how-eu-can-survive-in-geopolitical-age-pub-81132.